Testimony
Before the Committee on Oversight and Government Reform, House of Representatives

For Release on Delivery
Expected at 2:00 p.m. EDT
Tuesday, April 9, 2013

I0426043

GOVERNMENT EFFICIENCY AND EFFECTIVENESS

Opportunities to Reduce Fragmentation, Overlap, and Duplication and Achieve Other Financial Benefits

Statement of Gene L. Dodaro
Comptroller General of the United States

Chairman Issa, Ranking Member Cummings, and Members of the Committee:

Thank you for the opportunity to discuss our 2013 annual report, which presents 31 new opportunities to reduce fragmentation, overlap, and duplication as well as achieve other financial benefits. It also presents the results of our efforts to follow up on progress made by executive branch agencies and Congress in addressing the areas we identified in our 2011 and 2012 annual reports.[1] Through these three annual reports, we have completed a systematic examination to identify major instances of fragmentation, overlap, or duplication across the federal government. In light of today's challenging fiscal environment, we have also identified additional opportunities to achieve greater efficiency and effectiveness by means of cost savings or enhanced revenue collection.

My testimony today describes the (1) new areas identified in our 2013 annual report where fragmentation, overlap, or duplication exists among federal programs or activities, as well as other opportunities to achieve cost savings or enhanced revenue; (2) status of actions taken by executive branch agencies and Congress in addressing the 131 areas identified in our 2011 and 2012 annual reports; and (3) the summary results of our 3-year systematic examination across the federal government to identify major instances of fragmentation, overlap, or duplication. My comments are based upon our 2013 annual report, which is being released today. That report is based upon work GAO previously conducted in accordance with generally accepted government auditing standards.

In summary, our 2013 annual report identifies 31 new areas where agencies may be able to achieve greater efficiency or effectiveness. Within these 31 areas, we identify 81 actions that the executive branch or Congress could take to address the issues we identified. Although it may be appropriate for multiple agencies or entities to be involved in the same programmatic or policy area due to the nature or magnitude of the federal effort, our report includes 17 areas of fragmentation, overlap, or

---

[1]GAO, *Opportunities to Reduce Potential Duplication in Government Programs, Save Tax Dollars, and Enhance Revenue*, GAO-11-318SP (Washington, D.C.: Mar. 1, 2011); and *2012 Annual Report: Opportunities to Reduce Duplication, Overlap and Fragmentation, Achieve Savings, and Enhance Revenue*, GAO-12-342SP (Washington D.C.: Feb. 28, 2012).

duplication where multiple programs and activities may be creating inefficiencies. Figure 1 illustrates the definitions we use for fragmentation, overlap, and duplication for this work. The report also identifies 14 additional areas where opportunities exist to achieve cost savings or enhance revenue collections.

Figure 1: Definitions of Fragmentation, Overlap, and Duplication

Fragmentation refers to those circumstances in which more than one federal agency (or more than one organization within an agency) is involved in the same broad area of national need and opportunities exist to improve service delivery.

Overlap occurs when multiple agencies or programs have similar goals, engage in similar activities or strategies to achieve them, or target similar beneficiaries.

Duplication occurs when two or more agencies or programs are engaged in the same activities or provide the same services to the same beneficiaries.

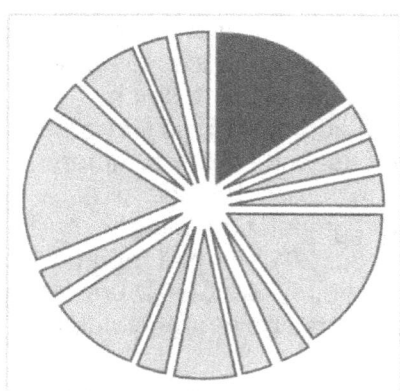 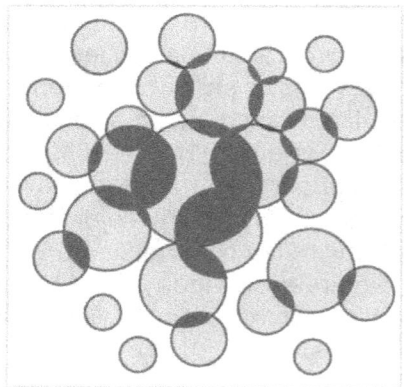 

Source: GAO.

The executive branch and Congress have made some progress in addressing the areas that we previously identified. In our 2011 and 2012 annual reports, we identified approximately 300 actions among 131 overall areas that the executive branch and Congress could take to reduce or eliminate fragmentation, overlap, or duplication or achieve other potential financial benefits. As of March 6, 2013, the date we completed our progress update audit work, 16 of the 131 overall areas were addressed; 87 were partially addressed; and 27 were not addressed.[2] Within these areas, 65 of the approximately 300 individual actions were addressed.[3] However, 149 actions were partially addressed and 85 actions remain not addressed, highlighting the need for sustained attention and leadership.[4]

Through our three annual reports, we have identified 162 areas in which there are opportunities to reduce fragmentation, overlap, or duplication or to achieve cost savings or enhance revenue. (Appendix I presents a summary of the areas we identified in our three annual reports.) Within these 162 areas, we identify approximately 380 actions that the executive branch or Congress could take to address the issues we identified. These areas span a wide range of government missions, covering activities within all 15 cabinet-level executive departments and 17 other federal entities. Collectively, if the actions we suggest are implemented, the government could potentially save tens of billions of dollars annually.

---

[2]In assessing progress on the 81 areas we identified in our 2011 annual report for this year's report, we combined two areas related to the Department of Homeland Security's management of acquisitions (Areas 75 and 76) into one area. Therefore, we are evaluating progress for 80 areas identified in our 2011 annual report and 51 areas identified in our 2012 annual report. In assessing overall progress for an area, we determined that an area was "addressed" if all actions in that area were addressed; "partially addressed" if at least one action needed in that area showed some progress toward implementation but not all actions were addressed; and "not addressed" if none of the actions needed in that area was addressed or partially addressed.

[3]For congressional actions, we applied the following criteria: "addressed" means relevant legislation has been enacted; "partially addressed" means a relevant bill has passed a committee, the House of Representatives, or the Senate, or relevant legislation only addressed part of the action needed; and "not addressed" means a bill may have been introduced but did not pass out of a committee, or no relevant legislation has been introduced. For executive branch actions, "addressed" means implementation of the action needed has been completed; "partially addressed" means a response to the action needed is in development, but not yet completed; and "not addressed" means that minimal or no progress has been made toward implementing the action needed.

[4]We are not assessing 9 actions this year that were previously included in our 2011 and 2012 reports. Based on subsequent audit work that we conducted, these actions have been consolidated, redirected from a congressional to an executive branch action, or revised to reflect updated information or data that we obtained. Further, 16 actions reported in 2011 and 2012 were revised this year due to additional audit work or other information we considered.

2013 Annual Report Identifies 31 New Areas Where Opportunities Exist to Achieve Greater Efficiency or Effectiveness

In 17 of the 31 new areas where agencies may be able to achieve greater efficiency or effectiveness, we found evidence of fragmentation, overlap, or duplication among federal programs or activities. As described in table 1, these programs or activities cover a wide range of federal functions and missions.

Table 1: Fragmentation, Overlap, and Duplication Areas Identified in Our 2013 Annual Report, by Mission

Mission	Areas Identified
Agriculture	1. **Catfish Inspection:** Repealing provisions of the 2008 Farm Bill that assigned U.S. Department of Agriculture's Food Safety and Inspection Service responsibility for examining and inspecting catfish and for creating a catfish inspection program would avoid duplication of already existing federal programs and could save taxpayers millions of dollars annually without affecting the safety of catfish intended for human consumption.
Defense	2. **Combat Uniforms:** The Department of Defense's fragmented approach to developing and acquiring uniforms could be more efficient, better protect service members, and result in up to $82 million in development and acquisition cost savings through increased collaboration among the military services.
	3. **Defense Foreign Language Support Contracts:** The Department of Defense should address fragmentation in the department's acquisition approach for foreign language support contracts, which are estimated to cost more than $1 billion annually, by exploring opportunities to gain additional efficiencies.
Energy	4. **Renewable Energy Initiatives:** Federal support for wind and solar energy, biofuels, and other renewable energy sources, which has been estimated at several billion dollars per year, is fragmented because 23 agencies implemented hundreds of renewable energy initiatives in fiscal year 2010—the latest year for which GAO developed these original data. Further, the Departments of Energy and Agriculture could take additional actions—to the extent possible within their statutory authority—to help ensure effective use of financial support from several wind initiatives, which GAO found provided duplicative support that may not have been needed in all cases for projects to be built.
Health	5. **Joint Veterans and Defense Health Care Services:** The Departments of Veterans Affairs and Defense should enhance their collaboration to reduce costs, overlap, and potential duplication in the delivery of health care services between two of the nation's largest health care systems that together provide health care to nearly 16 million veterans, service members, military retirees, and other beneficiaries.
	6. **Medicaid Program Integrity:** The Centers for Medicare & Medicaid Services needs to take steps to eliminate duplication and increase efficiency in two Medicaid Integrity Program activities—provider audits and the collection of state program integrity data.
Homeland security/law enforcement	7. **Department of Homeland Security Research and Development:** Better policies and guidance for defining, overseeing, and coordinating research and development investments and activities would help the Department of Homeland Security address fragmentation, overlap, and potential unnecessary duplication.

Mission	Areas Identified
	8. **Field-Based Information Sharing:** To help reduce inefficiencies resulting from overlap in analytical and investigative support activities, the Departments of Justice and Homeland Security and the Office of National Drug Control Policy could improve coordination among five types of field-based information sharing entities that may collect, process, analyze, or disseminate information in support of law-enforcement and counterterrorism-related efforts—Joint Terrorism Task Forces, Field Intelligence Groups, Regional Information Sharing Systems centers, state and major urban area fusion centers, and High Intensity Drug Trafficking Areas Investigative Support Centers.
	9. **Justice and Treasury Asset Forfeiture:** Conducting a study to evaluate the feasibility of consolidating the Departments of Justice's and Treasury's multimillion dollar asset forfeiture activities could help the departments identify the extent to which consolidation of potentially duplicative activities would help increase the efficiency and effectiveness of the programs and achieve cost savings.
Information technology	10. **Dissemination of Technical Research Reports:** Congress may wish to consider whether the fee-based model under which the National Technical Information Service currently operates for disseminating technical information is still viable or appropriate, given that many of the reports overlap with similar information available from the issuing organizations or other sources for free.
	11. **Geospatial Investments:** Better coordination among federal agencies that collect, maintain, and use geospatial information could help reduce duplication of geospatial investments and provide the opportunity for potential savings of millions of dollars.
International affairs	12. **Export Promotion:** Enhanced collaboration between the Small Business Administration and two other agencies could help to limit overlapping export-related services for small businesses.
	13. **International Broadcasting:** The Broadcasting Board of Governors—with a budget of $752 million in fiscal year 2012—has recognized the need to reduce overlap and reallocate limited resources to broadcasts that will have the greatest impact, but the agency could do more to achieve this goal, such as systematically considering overlap of language services in its annual language services review.
Science and the environment	14. **Rural Water Infrastructure:** Additional coordination by the Environmental Protection Agency and the Department of Agriculture could help three water and wastewater infrastructure programs with combined funding of about $4.3 billion avoid potentially duplicative application requirements, as well as associated costs and time developing engineering reports and environmental analyses.
Social services	15. **Drug Abuse Prevention and Treatment Programs:** More fully assessing the extent of overlap and potential duplication across the fragmented 76 federal drug abuse prevention and treatment programs and identifying opportunities for increased coordination, including those programs where no coordination has occurred, would better position the Office of National Drug Control Policy to better leverage resources and increase efficiencies.
Training, employment, and education	16. **Higher Education Assistance:** Federal agencies providing assistance for higher education should better coordinate to improve program administration and help reduce fragmentation.
	17. **Veterans' Employment and Training:** The Departments of Labor, Veterans Affairs, and Defense need to better coordinate the employment services each provides to veterans, and Labor needs to better target the Disabled Veterans' Outreach Program so that it does not overlap with other programs.

Source: GAO.

We consider programs or activities to be fragmented when more than one federal agency (or more than one organization within an agency) is involved in the same broad area of national need and opportunities may exist to improve how the government delivers services. We identified fragmentation in multiple programs we reviewed, including the following:

- *Combat Uniforms:* We found that the Department of Defense's (DOD) fragmented approach to developing and acquiring uniforms could be more efficient. Since 2002, the military services have shifted from using two camouflage patterns to seven service-specific camouflage uniforms with varying patterns and colors. Although DOD established a board to help ensure collaboration and DOD-wide integration of clothing and textile activities, we continue to identify inefficiencies in DOD's uniform acquisition approach. For example, we found that none of the services had taken advantage of opportunities to reduce costs through partnering on inventory management or by collaborating to achieve greater standardization among their various camouflage uniforms. We have identified several actions DOD should take to realize potential efficiencies and up to $82 million in development and acquisition cost savings through increased collaboration among the military services. These actions include directing the Secretaries of the military departments to actively pursue partnerships for the joint development and use of uniforms.

- *Defense Foreign Language Support Contracts:* DOD obligated over $6.8 billion from fiscal years 2008 through 2012 on contracts to acquire a range of foreign language services and products, such as translation and interpretation services. Although the department has gained some efficiencies by centralizing contracting for certain services under an executive agent, it has not taken steps to comprehensively assess whether additional opportunities exist to gain efficiencies in the department's fragmented acquisition approach for foreign language support contracts. For example, we found that 159 contracting organizations in 10 different DOD components obligated approximately $1.2 billion on contracts outside of those managed by the executive agent, resulting in an uncoordinated and fragmented approach. Our prior work has found that agencies, including DOD, reported savings ranging between 5 and 20 percent by implementing more coordinated acquisition approaches rather than fragmented contracting. Given the department's level of obligations for foreign language support services, DOD could achieve significant cost savings by assessing and addressing the fragmentation in its current approach for managing these contracts.

- *Renewable Energy Initiatives:* Federal support for wind and solar energy, biofuels, and other renewable energy sources has increased significantly in recent years. Specifically, third-party estimates indicate that federal spending over the 7-year period from 2002 through 2008 averaged about $4 billion per year and increased to almost $15 billion in fiscal year 2010, in part because of additional spending through the American Recovery and Reinvestment Act of 2009. We found that federal support for renewable energy is fragmented, as 23 agencies and their 130 subagencies implemented hundreds of initiatives in fiscal year 2010.[5] We could not comprehensively assess the potential for overlap or duplication among these nearly 700 renewable energy initiatives, because existing agency information was not sufficiently complete to allow for such an assessment. However, fragmentation can be a harbinger of potential overlap or duplication. For example, we assessed federal wind energy initiatives and found that 82 wind-related initiatives that we examined had overlapping characteristics, and several of them have provided duplicative financial support to deploy wind energy projects. Such duplicative federal financial support may not have been needed in all cases for the projects to be built. To help ensure effective use of financial support, we suggested that the Department of Energy (Energy) and the Department of Agriculture (USDA), to the extent possible within their statutory authority, assess and document whether the financial support of their initiatives is needed when considering applications.

In some areas where fragmentation exists, we also found evidence of overlap, which occurs when multiple agencies or programs have similar goals, engage in similar activities or strategies to achieve them, or target similar beneficiaries. We found overlap among federal programs or initiatives in a variety of areas such as joint veterans and defense health care services, export promotion activities, and veterans' employment and training programs, as well as the following:

- *Department of Homeland Security Research and Development:* Within the Department of Homeland Security (DHS), we found six department components involved in research and development (R&D) activities. We examined 47 R&D contracts awarded by these components and found 35 instances among 29 contracts in which the contracts overlapped with activities conducted elsewhere in the department. Taken together, these 29 contracts were worth about $66 million. In one example of the overlap, we found that two DHS components awarded five separate contracts that each addressed detection of the same chemical. While we did not identify instances of

---

[5]We defined a renewable energy-related initiative as a program, tax expenditure, or group of activities serving a similar purpose or function that was related to renewable energy through a specific emphasis or focus, even if renewable energy was part of a broader effort. There is no comprehensive database that tracks federal renewable energy spending across agencies for all types of activities. Fiscal year 2010 is the latest year for which we developed original data on the renewable energy initiatives.

unnecessary duplication among these contracts, DHS has not developed a policy defining who is responsible for coordinating R&D and what processes should be used to coordinate it, and does not have mechanisms to track all R&D activities at DHS that could help prevent overlap, fragmentation, or unnecessary duplication. We suggested that developing a policy defining the roles and responsibilities for coordinating R&D, and establishing coordination processes and a mechanism to track all R&D projects could help DHS mitigate existing fragmentation and overlap, and reduce the risk of unnecessary duplication.

- *Drug Abuse Prevention and Treatment Programs:* In fiscal year 2012, about $4.5 billion was allocated to 15 federal agencies that administer 76 fragmented programs intended to prevent or treat illicit drug use or abuse. Of the 76 drug abuse prevention and treatment programs we reviewed, we also found evidence of overlap across 59 programs (nearly 80 percent). The Office of National Drug Control Policy (ONDCP) is responsible for overseeing and coordinating the implementation of drug abuse prevention and treatment program activities across the federal government. Although ONDCP has taken some steps to coordinate these activities, it has not systematically assessed drug abuse prevention and treatment programs to examine the extent of overlap and potential for duplication or to identify opportunities for greater coordination. Such an assessment would better position ONDCP to help ensure that federal agencies undertaking similar prevention and treatment efforts identify opportunities for increased efficiencies.

Overlap and fragmentation among government programs or activities can lead to duplication, which occurs when two or more agencies or programs are engaged in the same activities or provide the same services to the same beneficiaries. Our 2013 report includes several areas where we identified potentially duplicative federal efforts, including the following:

- *Catfish Inspection:* We found that when USDA's Food Safety and Inspection Service (FSIS) begins the catfish inspection program as mandated in the Food, Conservation, and Energy Act of 2008, the program will duplicate work already conducted by the Food and Drug Administration (FDA) and by the National Marine Fisheries Service. For example, as many as three agencies—FDA, FSIS, and the National Marine Fisheries Service—could inspect facilities that process both catfish and other types of seafood. To avoid this duplication, we suggest that Congress repeal the provisions of the act that assigned USDA responsibilities for examining and inspecting catfish and establishing a catfish inspection program. Taking this action could save taxpayers millions annually, according to FSIS estimates of the program's cost.[6]

- *Medicaid Program Integrity:* We also identified duplication in the Medicaid Integrity Program, which provides federal support and oversight of state programs.[7] Specifically, we identified duplication in two integrity program activities: (1) the National Medicaid Audit Program, which consists of audits of state Medicaid claims data to identify overpayments; and (2) state program integrity assessments, one of several tools through which the Centers for Medicare & Medicaid Services (CMS) collects data on state program integrity activities. For example, we found that the data collected through state program integrity assessments duplicate data collected through triennial comprehensive reviews and other reports, which provide more timely and useful information. We suggested that CMS merge certain functions of the federal review and audit contractors and discontinue the annual state program integrity assessment to eliminate or avoid duplicative activities.

- *Geospatial Investments:* According to the Department of the Interior, the federal government invests billions of dollars annually to collect, maintain, and use geospatial information—information linked to specific geographic locations that supports many government functions, such as maintaining roads and responding to natural disasters. We found that federal agencies had not effectively

---

[6]To create this potential savings, Congress would need to repeal the provision in the Food, Conservation, and Energy Act of 2008, or direct in the Food Safety and Inspection Service's appropriation that no funds may be spent on the program. If Congress enacts a legislative restriction, there may be some opportunity to rescind appropriated amounts. Because the inspection program is funded from a lump sum appropriation to USDA, funds that would have been used for the program could be available for new obligations within the appropriations account. USDA could identify the amount of funds currently available for obligation that would have been used for the catfish inspection program and Congress could rescind those amounts.

[7]Medicaid is the joint federal-state health care financing program for certain low-income individuals and is one of the largest social programs in federal and state budgets. We have had long-standing concerns about Medicaid's program integrity because of problems with the sufficiency of federal and state oversight. For example, the Centers for Medicare & Medicaid Services estimated that in fiscal year 2012, $19.2 billion (7.1 percent) of Medicaid's federal expenditures involved improper payments.

implemented policies and procedures that would help them to identify and coordinate geospatial data acquisitions across the government. For example, although the Office of Management and Budget (OMB) has oversight responsibilities for investments in geospatial data, OMB staff members acknowledged that OMB does not have complete and reliable information to identify potentially duplicative geospatial investments. According to these officials, this lack of information is largely because agencies do not appropriately and consistently classify geospatial investments in their budget documents submitted to OMB. As a result, the agencies make duplicative investments and risk missing opportunities to jointly acquire data. Better coordination by agencies and better oversight by OMB could help to reduce duplication of geospatial investments, providing the opportunity for potential savings of millions of dollars on geospatial information technology.

In addition to areas of fragmentation, overlap, and duplication, our 2013 annual report identified 14 areas where opportunities exist either to reduce the cost of government operations or enhance revenue collections for the Treasury. These opportunities for executive branch or congressional action exist in a wide range of federal government missions (see table 2).

Table 2: Cost Savings and Revenue Enhancement Opportunities Identified in Our 2013 Annual Report, by Mission

Mission	Areas Identified
Agriculture	18. **Agricultural Quarantine Inspection Fees**: The United States Department of Agriculture's Animal and Plant Health Inspection Service could have achieved as much as $325 million in savings (based on fiscal year 2011 data, as reported in GAO's March 2013 report) by more fully aligning fees with program costs; although the savings would be recurring, the amount would depend on the cost-collections gap in a given fiscal year and would result in a reduced reliance on U.S. Customs and Border Protection's annual Salaries and Expenses appropriations used for agricultural inspection services.
	19. **Crop Insurance**: To achieve up to $1.2 billion per year in cost savings in the federal crop insurance program, Congress could consider limiting the subsidy for premiums that an individual farmer can receive each year, reducing the subsidy for all or high-income farmers participating in the program, or some combination of limiting and reducing these subsidies.
Defense	20. **Joint Basing**: The Department of Defense needs an implementation plan to guide joint bases to achieve millions of dollars in cost savings and efficiencies anticipated from combining support services at 26 installations located close to one another.
Energy	21. **Department of Energy's Isotope Program**: Assessing the value of isotopes to customers, and other factors such as prices of alternatives, may show that the Department of Energy could increase prices for isotopes that it sells to commercial customers to create cost savings by generating additional revenue.
General government	22. **Additional Opportunities to Improve Internal Revenue Service Enforcement of Tax Laws**: The Internal Revenue Service can realize cost savings and increase revenue collections by billions of dollars by, among other things, using more rigorous analyses to better allocate enforcement and other resources.

Mission	Areas Identified
	23. **Agencies' Use of Strategic Sourcing**: Selected agencies could better leverage their buying power and achieve additional savings by directing more procurement spending to existing strategically sourced contracts and further expanding strategic sourcing practices to their highest spending procurement categories—savings of one percent from selected agencies' procurement spending alone would equate to over $4 billion.
	24. **Opportunities to Help Reduce Government Satellite Program Costs**: Government agencies could achieve considerable cost savings on some missions by leveraging commercial spacecraft through innovative mechanisms such as hosted payload arrangements and sharing launch vehicle costs. Selected agencies have reported saving hundreds of millions of dollars to date from using these innovative mechanisms.
Health	25. **Medicare Prepayment Controls**: More widespread use of prepayment edits could reduce improper payments and achieve other cost savings for the Medicare program, as well as provide more consistent coverage nationwide.
	26. **Medicaid Supplemental Payments**: To improve the transparency of and accountability for certain high-risk Medicaid payments that annually total tens of billions of dollars, Congress should consider requiring the Centers for Medicare & Medicaid Services to take steps that would facilitate the agency's ability to oversee these payments, including identifying payments that are not used for Medicaid purposes or are otherwise inconsistent with Medicaid payment principles, which could lead to cost savings. GAO's analysis for providers for which data are available suggests that savings could be in the hundreds of millions, or billions, of dollars.
	27. **Medicare Advantage Quality Bonus Payment Demonstration**: Rather than implementing the Medicare Advantage quality bonus payment program specifically established by law, the Centers for Medicare & Medicaid Services is testing an alternative bonus payment structure under a broad demonstration authority through a 3-year demonstration that has design flaws, raises legal concerns, and is estimated to cost over $8 billion; about $2 billion could be saved if it were canceled for its last year, 2014.
Homeland security/law enforcement	28. **Checked Baggage Screening**: By reviewing the appropriateness of the federal cost share the Transportation Security Administration applies to agreements financing airport facility modification projects related to the installation of checked baggage screening systems, the Transportation Security Administration could, if a reduced cost share was deemed appropriate, achieve cost efficiencies and be positioned to install a greater number of optimal baggage screening systems than it currently anticipates.
Information technology	29. **Cloud computing**: Better planning of cloud-based computing solutions provides an opportunity for potential savings of millions of dollars.
	30. **Information Technology Operations and Maintenance**: Strengthening oversight of key federal agencies' major information technology investments in operations and maintenance provides opportunity for savings on billions in information technology investments.
International affairs	31. **Tobacco Taxes**: Federal revenue losses were as much as $615 million to $1.1 billion between April 2009 and 2011 because manufacturers and consumers substituted higher-taxed smoking tobacco products with similar lower-taxed products. To address future revenue losses, Congress should consider modifying tobacco tax rates to eliminate significant tax differentials between similar products.

Source: GAO.

Among the 14 areas of opportunity to reduce costs or enhance revenue identified in our 2013 annual report are the following examples of opportunities for executive branch agencies or Congress to take action to address the issues we reported:

- *Medicare Advantage Quality Bonus Payment Demonstration:* We report concerns about CMS's Medicare Advantage Quality Bonus Payment Demonstration, which was estimated to cost $8.35 billion over 10 years, most of which will be paid to plans with average performance. Medicare Advantage provides health care coverage through private health plans offered by organizations under contract with CMS. The agency's stated research goal for the demonstration is to test whether a modified bonus structure leads to larger and faster annual quality improvement for Medicare Advantage plans. We found that the demonstration's design precludes a credible evaluation of its effectiveness because it lacks an appropriate comparison group needed to isolate the demonstration's effects, and because the demonstration's bonus payments are based largely on plan performance that predates the demonstration. Based on these concerns, we suggest that Department of Health and Human Services (HHS) cancel the Medicare Advantage Quality Bonus Payment Demonstration. In addition, the demonstration's design raises legal concerns about whether it falls within HHS's demonstration authority. Although the demonstration is now in its second year, HHS still has an opportunity to achieve significant cost savings—about $2 billion, based on our analysis of CMS actuaries' estimates—if it cancels the demonstration for 2014.

- *Crop Insurance:* The federal government's crop insurance costs have increased in recent years—rising from an average of $3.1 billion per year from fiscal years 2000 through 2006 to an average of $7.6 billion per year from fiscal years 2007 through 2012—and are expected to increase further. These costs include subsidies to pay for part of a farmer's crop insurance premiums, which farmers can purchase to insure against certain losses for insurable crops they produce. Unlike many farm programs, the federal crop insurance program does not have statutory income and payment limits that apply to individual farmers and legal entities, including corporations. Congress could achieve up to $1.2 billion per year in cost savings by limiting the subsidy for premiums that an individual farmer can receive each year, reducing the subsidy for all or high-income farmers participating in the program, or some combination of both.

- *Information Technology Operations and Maintenance:* Of the $79 billion federal agencies budgeted for information technology (IT) in fiscal year 2011, $54 billion (about 69 percent) was reported to have been spent on the operations and maintenance of existing legacy IT systems—commonly referred to as steady state investments. However, many federal agencies are not performing analyses to determine whether or not their steady state systems are continuing to meet business and customer needs and are contributing to meeting the agencies' strategic goals, as called for by OMB guidance. We found that agencies did not conduct such an analysis on 52 of the 75 major existing information technology investments we reviewed. As a result, there is increased potential for these IT investments in operations and maintenance to result in waste and duplication. We suggest that agencies analyze all IT investments annually and report the results of their analyses to OMB. These actions could help agencies achieve cost savings by strengthening the oversight of their existing IT investments in operations and maintenance, resulting in the potential for billions of dollars in savings.

- *Opportunities to Help Reduce Government Satellite Program Costs:* In recent years, Congress has appropriated more than $25 billion a year to agencies for developing space systems.[8] To save money, several federal agencies are actively using or exploring nontraditional approaches to managing their space-based programs, such as hosting government instruments on commercial spacecraft and having multiple satellites share the same launch vehicle.[9] For example, DOD has two ongoing hosted payload pilot missions and has taken preliminary steps to develop a follow-on effort. According to DOD estimates, the commercial partnership has saved the department over $200 million. While these approaches hold promise for providing lower-cost access to space in the future, we identified a variety of technical, cultural, logistical, and legal and policy challenges. We identify actions that Congress may wish to consider to address these challenges and better take advantage of nontraditional approaches, such as authorizing agencies enhanced flexibility to acquire certain satellite services related to hosted payload and ride sharing arrangements, when appropriately planned and justified.

- *Medicaid Supplemental Payments:* Medicaid—the joint federal-state program that finances health care for certain low-income individuals—cost the federal government and states an estimated $410 billion in 2011.[10] States pay qualified health care providers for covered services delivered to Medicaid beneficiaries and obtain federal matching funds

---

[8]A space system can include multiple components such as satellites, ground control stations, terminals, and user equipment.

[9]Several federal agencies, including DOD, the National Aeronautics and Space Administration, the Federal Aviation Administration, the National Oceanic and Atmospheric Administration, and the U.S. Coast Guard, are actively using or beginning to look at these approaches in order to save costs.

[10]The 2011 cost figure represents combined federal and state Medicaid expenditures for provider services in fiscal year 2011 and does not include expenditures for administration.

for the federal share of these payments. We found that many states are making Medicaid payments to many providers that are far in excess of those providers' costs of providing Medicaid services. Specifically, in 2007, the most recent year for which these data were available, 39 states made payments to certain providers in excess of Medicaid costs by a total of about $2.7 billion. To improve the transparency of and accountability for certain high-risk Medicaid payments, we suggest that Congress consider requiring CMS to take steps that would facilitate the agency's ability to oversee these payments, including identifying payments that are not used for Medicaid purposes or are otherwise inconsistent with Medicaid payment principles. Such action could lead to cost savings in the hundreds of millions, or even billions, of dollars.

- *Agencies' Use of Strategic Sourcing:* Federal agencies could achieve significant cost savings annually by expanding and improving their use of strategic sourcing—an acquisition process that moves away from numerous individual procurement actions to a broader aggregated approach. For example, a reduction of 1 percent from selected agencies' procurement spending would equate to over $4 billion in savings.[11] To help control spending, OMB established a government-wide strategic sourcing program to address opportunities to strategically source commonly purchased products and services and eliminate duplication of efforts across agencies. However, the program has not yet targeted the products and services on which the government spends the most. Moreover, a lack of clear guidance on metrics for measuring success has hindered the management of ongoing strategic sourcing efforts across the federal government. Thus, we suggested that OMB issue updated government-wide guidance on calculating savings and establish metrics to measure progress toward goals. Doing so would position OMB to help federal agencies better implement strategic sourcing practices and maximize their ability to realize billions of dollars in potential savings annually. In December 2012, OMB provided new direction to agencies to improve strategic sourcing, but it is too early to tell how effectively those actions will be implemented.

---

[11]These selected agencies include DOD, DHS, Energy, and the Department of Veterans Affairs, which accounted for 80 percent of the $537 billion in federal procurement spending in fiscal year 2011.

- *Department of Energy's Isotope Program:* Opportunities may also exist for Energy to generate additional revenue by increasing the price for isotopes that it sells to commercial customers.[12] Energy's Isotope Development and Production for Research and Applications program (Isotope Program) sells isotopes to commercial customers for a variety of uses, such as medical procedures and radiation detection equipment. To achieve its mission, the Isotope Program relies on annual appropriations—almost $20 million in fiscal year 2012—and revenues from isotope sales. Although revenues from sales of isotopes alone totaled over $25 million in fiscal year 2012, we found that Energy may be forgoing revenue because it is not using thorough assessments to set prices for commercial isotopes. To improve the program's transparency in setting isotope prices and determine if opportunities exist to generate additional revenue, we suggest that Energy assess the prices it sets for commercial isotopes to determine if prices can be increased.

The Executive Branch and Congress Have Made Some Progress in Addressing the Areas That We Previously Identified

In addition to the new actions identified in our 2013 annual report, we have continued to monitor the progress that the executive branch agencies and Congress have made in addressing issues we identified in our 2011 and 2012 annual reports. In these reports, we identified approximately 300 actions that the executive branch and Congress could take to reduce or eliminate fragmentation, overlap, or duplication or achieve other potential financial benefits.[13]

We evaluated progress by determining an "overall assessment" rating for each area and an individual rating for each action within an area (see figs. 2 and 3). We found that executive branch agencies and Congress have made progress in addressing many of the 131 areas we identified in 2011 and 2012. As of March 6, 2013, the date we completed our audit work, 16 of the 131 areas were addressed; 87 were partially addressed; and 27

---

[12]Isotopes are varieties of a given chemical element with the same number of protons but different numbers of neutrons. For example, the helium-3 isotope, which is used in research and to detect neutrons in radiation detection equipment, has one less neutron than the helium-4 isotope, which is the helium isotope commonly used in party balloons.

[13]We are not assessing 9 actions this year that were previously included in our 2011 and 2012 reports. Based on subsequent audit work that we conducted, these actions have been consolidated, redirected from a congressional to an executive branch action, or revised to reflect updated information or data that we obtained. Further, 16 actions reported in 2011 and 2012 were revised this year due to additional audit work or other information we considered.

were not addressed. We also found that of the approximately 300 actions needed within these areas, 65 were addressed; 149 were partially addressed; and 85 were not addressed.

Figure 2: Assessment of 2011 and 2012 Areas, as of March 6, 2013

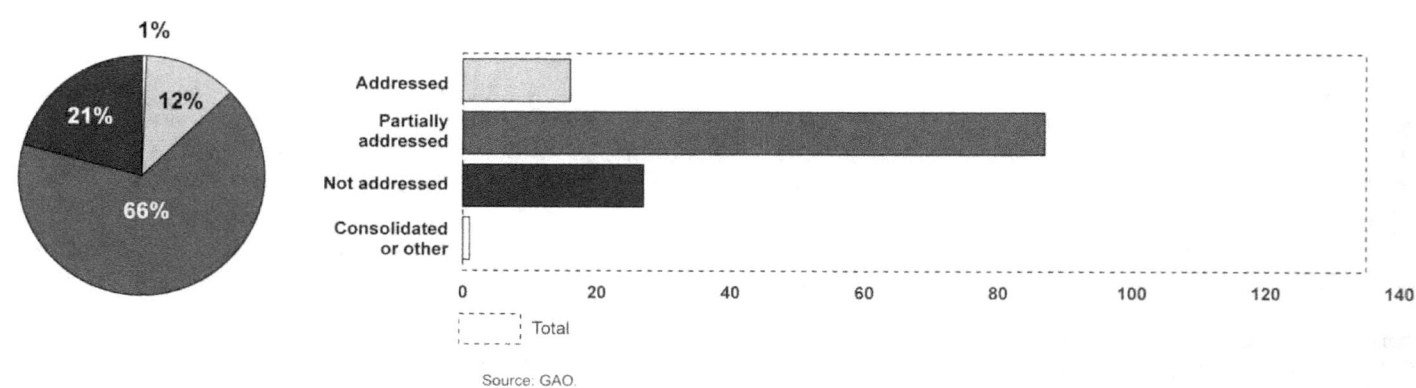

Source: GAO.

Note: In assessing overall progress for an area, we determined that an area was "addressed" if all actions in that area were addressed; "partially addressed" if at least one action needed in that area showed some progress toward implementation but not all actions were addressed; and "not addressed" if none of the actions needed in that area was addressed or partially addressed. The consolidated area was not assessed in 2013 due to additional work or other information we considered.

Figure 3: Assessment of 2011 and 2012 Actions, as of March 6, 2013

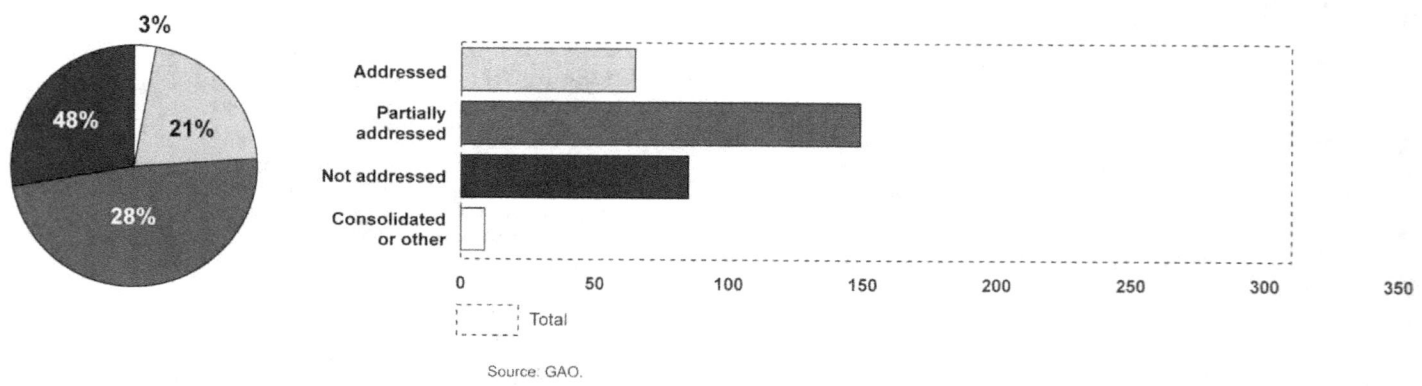

Source: GAO.

Note: In assessing actions suggested for Congress, we applied the following criteria: "addressed" means relevant legislation has been enacted and addresses all aspects of the action needed; "partially addressed" means a relevant bill has passed a committee, the House of Representatives, or the Senate, or relevant legislation has been enacted but only addressed part of the action needed; and "not addressed" means a bill may have been introduced but did not pass out of a committee, or no relevant legislation has been introduced. In assessing actions suggested for the executive branch, we applied the following criteria: "addressed" means implementation of the action needed has been completed; "partially addressed" means a response to the action needed is in development, or started but not yet completed; and "not addressed" means the administration, the agencies, or both have made minimal or no progress toward implementing the action needed. Consolidated actions were not assessed in 2013 due to additional work or other information we considered.

According to our analysis, 198 of the 249 actions (almost 80 percent) identified in 2011 and 2012 that were directed to executive branch agencies are either partially addressed or addressed. An example of the progress made is DOD's efforts to implement our suggested action related to the area of overseas defense posture. Specifically, in our 2012 annual report, we suggested the Secretary of Defense should direct appropriate organizations within DOD to complete a business case analysis, including an evaluation of alternative courses of action, for the strategic objectives that have to this point driven the decision to implement tour normalization in South Korea.[14] Based on the resulting business case analysis, DOD officials stated that United States Forces Korea determined that the tour normalization initiative was not affordable. This decision not to move forward with the tour normalization initiative resulted in cost avoidance of $3.1 billion from fiscal years 2012 through 2016.

Congress has also addressed some of our suggested actions—16 of the 50 actions directed to Congress in our 2011 and 2012 annual reports are either partially addressed or addressed (32 percent). For example, in our 2011 annual report, we stated that Congress could reduce revenue losses by more than $5.7 billion annually by addressing duplicative federal efforts directed at increasing domestic ethanol production. To reduce these revenue losses, we suggested that Congress consider whether revisions to the ethanol tax credit were needed, and we suggested options to consider, including allowing the volumetric ethanol excise tax credit to expire at the end of 2011. Congress addressed this suggested action by allowing the tax credit to expire at the end of 2011, which ended the ethanol tax credit for fuel blenders that purchase and blend ethanol with gasoline.

---

[14]Tour normalization refers to the initiative to extend the tour length of military service members and move thousands of dependents to South Korea.

Although the executive branch and Congress have made some progress in addressing the issues that we have previously identified, additional steps are needed to address the remaining areas to achieve associated benefits. A number of the issues are difficult to address, and implementing many of the actions identified will take time and sustained leadership. Nevertheless, implementing the actions could potentially save the government tens of billions of dollars annually. Appendix II highlights opportunities for potential financial benefits from our body of work.

To help maintain attention on these issues, we are concurrently releasing *GAO's Action Tracker*, a publicly accessible website of the 162 areas and approximately 380 suggested actions presented in our 2011, 2012, and 2013 reports. *GAO's Action Tracker* includes progress updates and assessments of legislative and executive branch actions needed. We will add areas and suggested actions identified in future reports to *GAO's Action Tracker* and periodically update the status of all identified areas and activities.

Over 3 Years, GAO Has Identified 162 Areas Where Federal Programs Could Achieve Greater Efficiency or Increase Effectiveness

Through our three annual reports, we have identified a total of 162 areas with actions that the executive branch and Congress could take to address fragmentation, overlap, and duplication or achieve cost savings. These three reports touch on areas in virtually all major federal departments and agencies. Specifically, the reports collectively identify opportunities to reduce fragmentation, overlap, and duplication or achieve other financial benefits within all 15 cabinet-level executive departments and at least 17 other federal entities. Figure 4 illustrates actions needed that we directed to federal departments and agencies in our three annual reports. As the figure shows, we have directed numerous actions to large federal departments and agencies that represent the majority of federal obligations, including 90 actions directed to DOD, 51 to Treasury, and 44 to HHS. These three agencies alone represented 56 percent of fiscal year 2011 obligations.

Figure 4: Actions Needed Directed to Federal Departments and Agencies in 2011-2013 Annual Reports

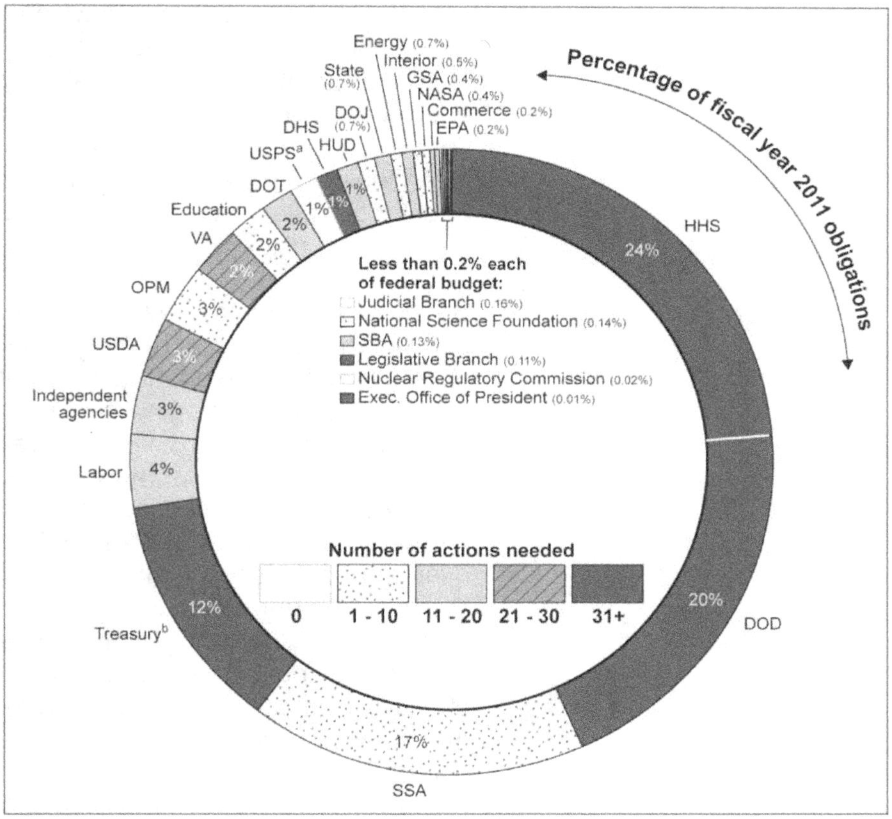

Percentage of fiscal year 2011 obligations

Energy (0.7%)
Interior (0.5%)
State (0.7%)
GSA (0.4%)
NASA (0.4%)
DOJ (0.7%)
Commerce (0.2%)
DHS
HUD
EPA (0.2%)
USPS[a]
DOT
Education
VA
OPM
USDA
Independent agencies
Labor
Treasury[b]

1%
1%
2%
2%
2%
3%
3%
3%
4%
12%

HHS 24%
DOD 20%
SSA 17%

Less than 0.2% each of federal budget:
Judicial Branch (0.16%)
National Science Foundation (0.14%)
SBA (0.13%)
Legislative Branch (0.11%)
Nuclear Regulatory Commission (0.02%)
Exec. Office of President (0.01%)

Number of actions needed

| 0 | 1 - 10 | 11 - 20 | 21 - 30 | 31+ |

Source: GAO.

[a]U.S. Postal Service (USPS) obligations are primarily funded by postal revenues, although USPS receives minimal appropriations for overseas voting and mail for the blind. Additionally, USPS has a maximum $15 billion in borrowing authority, which it reached in fiscal year 2012.

[b]Treasury's percentage of fiscal year 2011 obligations includes interest on the national debt.

Note: Individual actions needed are counted multiple times when they are directed to more than one federal department or agency.

Our 2013 annual report completes our 3-year systematic examination across the federal government to identify major instances of fragmentation, overlap, or duplication. Our systematic examination required a multiphased approach. First, we reviewed the budget functions of the federal government representing nearly all of the overall federal funds obligated in fiscal year 2010.[15] Federal budget functions classify budget resources by national need (such as National Defense, Energy, or Agriculture), and instances in which multiple federal agencies obligate funds within a particular budget function may indicate potential duplication or cost savings opportunities. Although this type of analysis cannot answer the question of whether overlap or duplication exists, it can help in the selection of areas for further investigation. Using this information, we identified each instance in which an executive branch or independent agency obligated more than $10 million within these 18 budget functions for further consideration.

Second, we reviewed key agency documents, such as strategic plans, performance and accountability reports, and budget justifications, as we have found that when multiple executive branch agencies have similar missions, goals, or programs, the potential for fragmentation, overlap, or duplication exists. Third, we reviewed key external published sources of information. In particular, we reviewed reports published by the Congressional Budget Office, Inspectors General, and the Congressional Research Service, as well as the President's budgets, to identify potential overlap and duplication among agency missions, goals, and programs. We relied on our previous work and professional judgment to target areas for further review by considering a variety of factors, including the extent of potential cost savings; opportunities for enhanced program efficiency or effectiveness; the degree to which multiple programs may be fragmented, overlapping, or duplicative; whether issues had been identified by GAO or external sources; and the level of coordination among agency programs.

Based on our multiphased approach, we have identified, to date, 162 areas in which there are opportunities to reduce fragmentation, overlap, or duplication or to achieve cost savings or revenue enhancement. Our three annual reports provide extensive coverage of major instances of fragmentation, overlap, or duplication across the federal government. Moving forward, we plan to perform further analysis to identify any other potential or emerging instances that may result in fragmentation, overlap, and duplication.

---

[15]Our examination did not include two budget functions: Allowances, because there were no actual obligations, and Undistributed Offsetting Receipts, because no obligations are charged to agencies.

In closing, as the fiscal pressures facing the nation continue, so too does the need for executive branch agencies and Congress to improve the efficiency and effectiveness of government programs and activities. Opportunities exist to improve the efficiency and effectiveness of government operations in the 162 areas we have included in our 2011-2013 annual reports.

Identifying, preventing, and addressing fragmentation, overlap, and duplication within the federal government is challenging. These are difficult issues to address because they may require agencies and Congress to re-examine within and across various mission areas the fundamental structure, operation, funding, and performance of a number of long-standing federal programs or activities with entrenched constituencies. Compounding these challenges is the lack of a comprehensive list of federal programs, reliable funding information, and regular performance information. Without knowing the full range of programs involved or the cost of implementing them, gauging the magnitude of the federal commitment to a particular area of activity or the extent to which associated federal programs are duplicative is difficult. Effective implementation of the Government Performance and Results Act of 1993 (GPRA) and the GPRA Modernization Act of 2010 could help address these challenges, as well as improve information sharing and coordination among federal agencies—both of which are needed to help address issues of fragmentation, overlap, and duplication.[16] The GPRA Modernization Act gave us a number of important reporting responsibilities, and through these responsibilities we will monitor the implementation of the act for Congress.

Furthermore, we plan to conduct further analysis to look for additional or emerging instances of fragmentation, overlap, and duplication and opportunities for cost savings or revenue enhancement. Likewise, we will continue to monitor developments in the areas we have already identified in this series. We stand ready to assist this and other committees in further analyzing the issues we have identified and evaluating potential solutions.

---

[16]Pub. L. No. 103-62, 107 Stat. 285 (1993); Pub. L. No. 111-352, 124 Stat. 3866 (2011).

Chairman Issa, Ranking Member Cummings, and Members of the Committee, this concludes my prepared statement. I would be pleased to answer questions.

GAO Contacts

For further information on this testimony or our April 9, 2013, report, please contact Orice Williams Brown, Managing Director, Financial Markets and Community Investment, who may be reached at (202) 512-8678 or williamso@gao.gov, and A. Nicole Clowers, Director, Financial Markets and Community Investment, who may be reached at (202) 512-8678 or clowersa@gao.gov. Contact points for the individual areas listed in our 2013 annual report can be found at the end of each area at http://www.gao.gov/products/GAO-13-279SP. Contact points for our Congressional Relations and Public Affairs offices may be found on the last page of this statement.

Appendix I: All Areas Identified in 2011-2013 Annual Reports, by Mission

This appendix summarizes all 162 areas we identified in our annual reports for 2011 through 2013. For areas included in our 2011 and 2012 reports, we also include our assessment of the overall progress made, as of March 6, 2013, in addressing the issues we identified. Table 3 presents areas related to fragmentation, overlap, and duplication. Table 4 presents areas related to cost savings or revenue enhancement.

Table 3: GAO Identified Areas of Fragmentation, Overlap, and Duplication in 2011-2013 Annual Reports

Mission	Annual report	Areas identified	Overall assessment
Agriculture	2011	Area 1: Fragmented **food safety** system has caused inconsistent oversight, ineffective coordination, and inefficient use of resources.	◑
	2012	Area 1: **Protection of Food and Agriculture**: Centrally coordinated oversight is needed to ensure more than nine federal agencies effectively and efficiently implement the nation's fragmented policy to defend the food and agriculture systems against potential terrorist attacks and major disasters.	◑
	2013	Area 1: **Catfish Inspection**: Repealing provisions of the 2008 Farm Bill that assigned U.S. Department of Agriculture's Food Safety and Inspection Service responsibility for examining and inspecting catfish and for creating a catfish inspection program would avoid duplication of already existing federal programs and could save taxpayers millions of dollars annually without affecting the safety of catfish intended for human consumption.	a
Defense	2011	Area 2: Realigning the **Department of Defense's** (DOD) **military medical command** structures and consolidating common functions could increase efficiency and result in projected savings ranging from $281 million to $460 million annually.	◑
	2011	Area 3: Opportunities exist for consolidation and increased efficiencies to maximize response to **warfighter urgent needs**.	◑
	2011	Area 4: Opportunities exist to avoid unnecessary redundancies and improve the coordination of **counter-improvised explosive device efforts**.	◑
	2011	Area 5: Opportunities exist to avoid unnecessary redundancies and maximize the efficient use of **intelligence, surveillance, and reconnaissance** capabilities.	◑
	2011	Area 6: A department-wide acquisition strategy could reduce DOD's risk of costly duplication in purchasing **Tactical Wheeled Vehicles**.	◑
	2011	Area 7: Improved joint oversight of DOD's **propositioning programs** for equipment and supplies may reduce unnecessary duplication.	◑
	2011	Area 8: **DOD's business systems modernization**: opportunities exist for optimizing business operations and systems.	◑
	2012	Area 2: **Electronic Warfare**: Identifying opportunities to consolidate DOD airborne electronic attack programs could reduce overlap in the department's multiple efforts to develop new capabilities and improve the department's return on its multibillion-dollar acquisition investments.	◑

Mission	Annual report	Areas identified	Overall assessment
	2012	Area 3: **Unmanned Aircraft Systems**: Ineffective acquisition practices and collaboration efforts in the DOD unmanned aircraft systems portfolio creates overlap and the potential for duplication among a number of current programs and systems.	
	2012	Area 4: **Counter-Improvised Explosive Device Efforts**: DOD continues to risk duplication in its multibillion-dollar counter Improvised Explosive Device efforts because it does not have a comprehensive database of its projects and initiatives.	
	2012	Area 5: **Defense Language and Culture Training**: DOD needs a more integrated approach to reduce fragmentation in training approaches and overlap in the content of training products acquired by the military services and other organizations.	
	2012	Area 6: **Stabilization, Reconstruction, and Humanitarian Assistance Efforts**: Improving the DOD's evaluations of stabilization, reconstruction, and humanitarian assistance efforts, and addressing coordination challenges with the Department of State (State) and the U.S. Agency for International Development (USAID), could reduce overlapping efforts and result in the more efficient use of taxpayer dollars.	
	2013	Area 2: **Combat Uniforms**: The Department of Defense's fragmented approach to developing and acquiring uniforms could be more efficient, better protect service members, and result in up to $82 million in development and acquisition cost savings through increased collaboration among the military services.	a
	2013	Area 3: **Defense Foreign Language Support Contracts**: The Department of Defense should address fragmentation in the department's acquisition approach for foreign language support contracts, which are estimated to cost more than $1 billion annually, by exploring opportunities to gain additional efficiencies.	a
Economic development	2011	Area 9: The efficiency and effectiveness of fragmented **economic development programs** are unclear.	
	2011	Area 10: The federal approach to **surface transportation** is fragmented, lacks clear goals, and is not accountable for results.	
	2011	Area 11: Fragmented federal efforts to meet **water needs** in the **U.S.-Mexico border region** have resulted in an administrative burden, redundant activities, and an overall inefficient use of resources.	
	2012	Area 7: **Support for Entrepreneurs**: Overlap and fragmentation among the economic development programs that support entrepreneurial efforts require the Office of Management and Budget (OMB) and other agencies to better evaluate the programs and explore opportunities for program restructuring, which may include consolidation, within and across agencies.	
	2012	Area 8: **Surface Freight Transportation**: Fragmented federal programs and funding structures are not maximizing the efficient movement of freight.	
Energy	2011	Area 12: Resolving conflicting requirements could more effectively achieve **federal fleet energy goals**.	
	2011	Area 13: Addressing duplicative federal efforts directed at increasing **domestic ethanol production** could reduce revenue losses by more than $5.7 billion annually.	

Mission	Annual report	Areas identified	Overall assessment
	2012	Area 9: **Department of Energy Contractor Support Costs**: The Department of Energy (DOE) should assess whether further opportunities could be taken to streamline support functions, estimated to cost over $5 billion, at its contractor-managed laboratory and nuclear production and testing sites, in light of contractors' historically fragmented approach to providing these functions.	●
	2012	Area 10: **Nuclear Nonproliferation**: Comprehensive review needed to address strategic planning limitations and potential fragmentation and overlap concerns among programs combating nuclear smuggling overseas.	○
	2013	Area 4: **Renewable Energy Initiatives**: Federal support for wind and solar energy, biofuels, and other renewable energy sources, which has been estimated at several billion dollars per year, is fragmented because 23 agencies implemented hundreds of renewable energy initiatives in fiscal year 2010—the latest year for which GAO developed these original data. Further, the DOE and USDA could take additional actions—to the extent possible within their statutory authority—to help ensure effective use of financial support from several wind initiatives, which GAO found provided duplicative support that may not have been needed in all cases for projects to be built.	a
General government	2011	Area 14: **Enterprise architectures**: key mechanisms for identifying potential overlap and duplication.	◑
	2011	Area 15: Consolidating **federal data** centers provides opportunity to improve government efficiency.	◑
	2011	Area 16: Collecting improved data on **interagency contracting** to minimize duplication could help the government leverage its vast buying power.	◑
	2011	Area 17: Periodic reviews could help ineffective **tax expenditures** and redundancies in related tax and spending programs, potentially reducing revenue losses by billions of dollars.	◑
	2012	Area 11: **Personnel Background Investigations**: The Office of Management and Budget (OMB) should take action to prevent agencies from making potentially duplicative investments in electronic case management and adjudication systems.	○
	2012	Area 12: **Cybersecurity Human Capital**: Government-wide initiatives to enhance cybersecurity workforce in the federal government need better structure, planning, guidance, and coordination to reduce duplication.	◑
	2012	Area 13: **Spectrum Management**: Enhanced coordination of federal agencies' efforts to manage radio frequency spectrum and an examination of incentive mechanisms to foster more efficient spectrum use may aid regulators' attempts to jointly respond to competing demands for spectrum while identifying valuable spectrum that could be auctioned for commercial use, thereby generating revenues for the U.S. Department of Treasury (Treasury).	◑
Health	2011	Area 18: Opportunities exist for **DOD** and the **U.S. Department of Veterans Affairs (VA)** to jointly modernize their **electronic health records systems**.	◑
	2011	Area 19: **VA** and **DOD** need to control **drug** costs and increase **joint contracting** wherever it is cost-effective.	◑
	2011	Area 20: The U.S. Department of Health and Human Services (HHS) needs an overall strategy to better integrate nationwide **public health information** systems.	○

Mission	Annual report	Areas identified	Overall assessment
	2012	Area 14: **Health Research Funding**: The National Institutes of Health (NIH), DOD, and VA can improve sharing of information to help avoid the potential for unnecessary duplication.	◑
	2012	Area 15: **Military and Veterans Health Care**: DOD and VA need to improve integration across care coordination and case management programs to reduce duplication and better assist servicemembers, veterans, and their families.	◑
	2013	Area 5: **Joint Veterans and Defense Health Care Services**: The Departments of Veterans Affairs and Defense should enhance their collaboration to reduce costs, overlap, and potential duplication in the delivery of health care services between two of the nation's largest health care systems that together provide health care to nearly 16 million veterans, service members, military retirees, and other beneficiaries.	a
	2013	Area 6: **Medicaid Program Integrity**: The Centers for Medicare & Medicaid Services needs to take steps to eliminate duplication and increase efficiency in two Medicaid Integrity Program activities—provider audits and the collection of state program integrity data.	a
Homeland security/law enforcement	2011	Area 21: Strategic oversight mechanisms could help integrate fragmented interagency efforts to defend against **biological threats**.	◑
	2011	Area 22: DHS oversight could help eliminate potential duplicating efforts of interagency forums in **securing** the **northern border**.	○
	2011	Area 23: The Department of Justice (DOJ) plans actions to reduce overlap in **explosives investigations**, but monitoring is needed to ensure successful implementation.	●
	2011	Area 24: **The Transportation Security Administration's (TSA) security assessments** on commercial trucking companies overlap with those of another agency, but efforts are under way to address the overlap.	◑
	2011	Area 25: DHS could streamline mechanisms **for sharing security-related information** with **public transit agencies** to help address overlapping information.	◑
	2011	Area 26: The **Federal Emergency Management Agency (FEMA)** needs to improve its oversight of **grants** and establish a framework for assessing capabilities to identify gaps and prioritize investments.	◑
	2012	Area 16: **Department of Justice Grants**: The Department of Justice could improve how it targets nearly $3.9 billion to reduce the risk of potential unnecessary duplication across the more than 11,000 grant awards it makes annually.	◑
	2012	Area 17: **Homeland Security Grants**: DHS needs better project information and coordination among four overlapping grant programs.	◑
	2012	Area 18: **Federal Facility Risk Assessments**: Agencies are making duplicate payments for facility risk assessments by completing their own assessments, while also paying DHS for assessments that the department is not performing.	◑
	2013	Area 7: **Department of Homeland Security Research and Development**: Better policies and guidance for defining, overseeing, and coordinating research and development investments and activities would help DHS address fragmentation, overlap, and potential unnecessary duplication.	a

Mission	Annual report	Areas identified	Overall assessment
	2013	Area 8: **Field-Based Information Sharing**: To help reduce inefficiencies resulting from overlap in analytical and investigative support activities, the Departments of Justice and Homeland Security and the Office of National Drug Control Policy could improve coordination among five types of field-based information sharing entities that may collect, process, analyze, or disseminate information in support of law enforcement and counterterrorism-related efforts—Joint Terrorism Task Forces, Field Intelligence Groups, Regional Information Sharing Systems centers, state and major urban area fusion centers, and High Intensity Drug Trafficking Areas Investigative Support Centers.	a
	2013	Area 9: **Justice and Treasury Asset Forfeiture**: Conducting a study to evaluate the feasibility of consolidating Justice's and Treasury's multimillion dollar asset forfeiture activities could help the departments identify the extent to which consolidation of potentially duplicative activities would help increase the efficiency and effectiveness of the programs and achieve cost savings.	a
Information technology	2012	Area 19: **Information Technology Investment Management**: OMB, and DOD and DOE need to address potentially duplicative information technology investments to avoid investing in unnecessary systems.	◑
	2013	Area 10: **Dissemination of Technical Research Reports**: Congress may wish to consider whether the fee-based model under which the National Technical Information Service currently operates for disseminating technical information is still viable or appropriate, given that many of the reports overlap with similar information available from the issuing organizations or other sources for free.	a
	2013	Area 11: **Geospatial Investments**: Better coordination among federal agencies that collect, maintain, and use geospatial information could help reduce duplication of geospatial investments and provide the opportunity for potential savings of millions of dollars.	a
International affairs	2011	Area 27: Lack of information sharing could create the potential for duplication of efforts between U.S. agencies involved in **development efforts** in **Afghanistan**.	◑
	2011	Area 28: Despite restructuring, overlapping roles and functions still exist at State's **Arms Control** and **Nonproliferation Bureaus**.	●
	2012	Area 20: **Overseas Administrative Services**: U.S. government agencies could lower the administrative cost of their operations overseas by increasing participation in the International Cooperative Administrative Support Services system and by reducing reliance on American officials overseas to provide these services.	◑
	2012	Area 21: **Training to Identify Fraudulent Travel Documents**: Establishing a formal coordination mechanism could help reduce duplicative activities among seven different entities that are involved in training foreign officials to identify fraudulent travel documents.	○
	2013	Area 12: **Export Promotion**: Enhanced collaboration between the Small Business Administration (SBA) and two other agencies could help to limit overlapping export-related services for small businesses.	a
	2013	Area 13: **International Broadcasting**: The Broadcasting Board of Governors—with a budget of $752 million in fiscal year 2012—has recognized the need to reduce overlap and reallocate limited resources to broadcasts that will have the greatest impact, but the agency could do more to achieve this goal, such as systematically considering overlap of language services in its annual language services review.	a

Mission	Annual report	Areas identified	Overall assessment
Science and the environment	2012	Area 22: **Coordination of Space System Organizations**: Fragmented leadership has led to program challenges and potential duplication in developing multibillion-dollar space systems.	◑
	2012	Area 23: **Space Launch Contract Costs**: Increased collaboration between the Department of Defense and the National Aeronautics and Space Administration could reduce launch contracting duplication.	◑
	2012	Area 24: **Diesel Emissions**: Fourteen grant and loan programs at DOE, Department of Transportation (DOT), and the Environmental Protection Agency (EPA), and three tax expenditures fund activities that have the effect of reducing mobile source diesel emissions; enhanced collaboration and performance measurement could improve these fragmented and overlapping programs.	○
	2012	Area 25: **Environmental Laboratories**: EPA needs to revise its overall approach to managing its 37 laboratories to address potential overlap and fragmentation and more fully leverage its limited resources.	◑
	2012	Area 26: **Green Building**: To evaluate the potential for overlap or fragmentation among federal green building initiatives, the Department of Housing and Urban Development, DOE, and EPA should lead other federal agencies in collaborating on assessing their investments in more than 90 initiatives to foster green building in the nonfederal sector.	◑
	2013	Area 14: **Rural Water Infrastructure**: Additional coordination by the EPA and the USDA could help three water and wastewater infrastructure programs with combined funding of about $4.3 billion avoid potentially duplicative application requirements, as well as associated costs and time developing engineering reports and environmental analyses.	a
Social services	2011	Area 29: Actions needed to reduce administrative overlap among **domestic food assistance** programs.	○
	2011	Area 30: Better coordination of federal **homelessness** programs may minimize fragmentation and overlap.	◑
	2011	Area 31: Further steps needed to improve cost-effectiveness and enhance services for **transportation-disadvantaged** persons.	◑
	2012	Area 27: **Social Security Benefit Coordination**: Benefit offsets for related programs help reduce the potential for overlapping payments but pose administrative challenges.	◑
	2012	Area 28: **Housing Assistance**: Examining the benefits and costs of housing programs and tax expenditures that address the same or similar populations or areas, and potentially consolidating them, could help mitigate overlap and fragmentation and decrease costs.	○
	2013	Area 15: **Drug Abuse Prevention and Treatment Programs**: More fully assessing the extent of overlap and potential duplication across the fragmented 76 federal drug abuse prevention and treatment programs and identifying opportunities for increased coordination, including those programs where no coordination has occurred, would better position the Office of National Drug Control Policy to better leverage resources and increase efficiencies.	a

Mission	Annual report	Areas identified	Overall assessment
Training, employment, and education	2011	Area 32: Multiple **employment** and **training** programs: providing information on colocating services and consolidating administrative structures could promote efficiencies.	◐
	2011	Area 33: **Teacher quality**: proliferation of programs complicates federal efforts to invest dollars effectively.	◐
	2011	Area 34: Fragmentation of **financial literacy** efforts makes coordination essential.	●
	2012	Area 29: **Early Learning and Child Care**: The Departments of Education and Health and Human Services (HHS) should extend their coordination efforts to other federal agencies with early learning and child care programs to mitigate the effects of program fragmentation, simplify children's access to these services, collect the data necessary to coordinate operation of these programs, and identify and minimize any unwarranted overlap and potential duplication.	◐
	2012	Area 30: **Employment for People with Disabilities**: Better coordination among 45 programs in nine federal agencies that support employment for people with disabilities could help mitigate program fragmentation and overlap, and reduce the potential for duplication or other inefficiencies.	◐
	2012	Area 31: **Science, Technology, Engineering, and Mathematics Education**: Strategic planning is needed to better manage overlapping programs across multiple agencies	◐
	2012	Area 32: **Financial Literacy**: Overlap among financial literacy activities makes coordination and clarification of roles and responsibilities essential, and suggests potential benefits of consolidation.	●
	2013	Area 16: **Higher Education Assistance**: Federal agencies providing assistance for higher education should better coordinate to improve program administration and help reduce fragmentation.	a
	2013	Area 17: **Veterans' Employment and Training**: The Departments of Labor, Veterans Affairs, and Defense need to better coordinate the employment services each provides to veterans, and Labor needs to better target the Disabled Veterans' Outreach Program so that it does not overlap with other programs.	a

Source: GAO analysis.

[a]As of April 9, 2013, we have not assessed the 2013 areas identified.

● = Addressed, meaning all actions needed in that area were addressed.

◐ = Partially addressed, meaning at least one action needed in that area showed some progress toward implementation, but not all actions were addressed.

○ = Not addressed, meaning none of the actions needed in that area were addressed or partially addressed.

Consolidated or other = actions were not assessed this year

Table 4: GAO Identified Areas of Cost-Savings and Revenue-Enhancement Opportunities in 2011-2013 Annual Reports

Mission	Annual report	Areas identified	Overall assessment
Agriculture	2011	Area 35: Reducing **farm program direct payments** could result in savings from $800 million over 10 years to up to $5 billion annually.	○
	2013	Area 18: **Agricultural Quarantine Inspection Fees:** The United States Department of Agriculture's Animal and Plant Health Inspection Service could have achieved as much as $325 million in savings (based on fiscal year 2011 data, as reported in GAO's March 2013 report) by more fully aligning fees with program costs; although the savings would be recurring, the amount would depend on the cost-collections gap in a given fiscal year and would result in a reduced reliance on U.S. Customs and Border Protection's annual Salaries and Expenses appropriations used for agricultural inspection services.	a
	2013	Area 19: **Crop Insurance:** To achieve up to $1.2 billion per year in cost savings in the federal crop insurance program, Congress could consider limiting the subsidy for premiums that an individual farmer can receive each year, reducing the subsidy for all or high-income farmers participating in the program, or some combination of limiting and reducing these subsidies.	a
Defense	2011	Area 36: DOD should assess costs and benefits of **overseas military presence** options before committing to costly personnel realignments and construction plans, thereby possibly saving billions of dollars.	◐
	2011	Area 37: Total compensation approach is needed to manage significant growth in **military personnel costs**.	◐
	2011	Area 38: Employing best management practices could help DOD save money on its **weapon systems acquisition programs**.	◐
	2011	Area 39: More efficient management could limit future costs of **DOD's spare parts inventory**.	◐
	2011	Area 40: More comprehensive and complete cost data can help DOD improve the cost-effectiveness of **sustaining weapons systems**.	◐
	2011	Area 41: Improved **corrosion prevention** and control practices could help DOD avoid billions in unnecessary costs over time.	◐
	2012	Area 33: **Air Force Food Service:** The Air Force has opportunities to achieve millions of dollars in cost savings annually by reviewing and renegotiating food service contracts, where appropriate, to better align with the needs of installations.	●
	2012	Area 34: **Defense Headquarters:** DOD should review and identify further opportunities for consolidating or reducing the size of headquarters organizations.	◐
	2012	Area 35: **Defense Real Property:** Ensuring the receipt of fair market value for leasing underused real property and monitoring administrative costs could help the military services' enhanced use lease programs realize intended financial benefits.	◐
	2012	Area 36: **Military Health Care Costs:** To help achieve significant projected cost savings and other performance goals, DOD needs to complete, implement, and monitor detailed plans for each of its approved health care initiatives.	◐

Mission	Annual report	Areas identified	Overall assessment
	2012	Area 37: **Overseas Defense Posture:** DOD could reduce costs of its Pacific region presence by developing comprehensive cost information and re-examining alternatives to planned initiatives.	◑
	2012	Area 38: **Navy's Information Technology Enterprise Network:** Better informed decisions are needed to ensure a more cost-effective acquisition approach for the U.S. Navy's Next Generation Enterprise Network.	○
	2013	Area 20: **Joint Basing:** DOD needs an implementation plan to guide joint bases to achieve millions of dollars in cost savings and efficiencies anticipated from combining support services at 26 installations located close to one another.	a
Economic development	2011	Area 42: Revising the **essential air service** program could improve efficiency.	◑
	2011	Area 43: Improved design and management of the **universal service fund** as it expands to support broadband could help avoid cost increases for consumers.	◑
	2011	Area 44: The U.S. Army **Corps of Engineers** should provide Congress with project-level information on unobligated balances.	●
	2012	Area 39: **Auto Recovery Office:** Unless the Secretary of Labor can demonstrate how the Auto Recovery Office has uniquely assisted auto communities, Congress may wish to consider prohibiting the Department of Labor from spending any of its appropriations on the Auto Recovery Office and instead require that the department direct the funds to other federal programs that provide funding directly to affected communities.	○
Energy	2011	Area 45: Improved management of federal **oil and gas resources** could result in approximately $2 billion in revenues over 10 years.	◑
	2012	Area 40: **Excess Uranium Inventories:** Marketing the Department of Energy's excess uranium could provide substantial revenue for the government.	○
	2013	Area 21: **Department of Energy's Isotope Program:** Assessing the value of isotopes to customers, and other factors such as prices of alternatives, may show that the Department of Energy could increase prices for isotopes that it sells to commercial customers to create cost savings by generating additional revenue.	a
General government	2011	Area 46: Efforts to address **government-wide improper payments** could result in significant costs savings.	◑
	2011	Area 47: Promoting **competition for** the over $500 billion in **federal contracts** could potentially save billions of dollars over time.	◑
	2011	Area 48: Applying **strategic sourcing** best practices throughout the federal procurement system could saves billions of dollars annually.	◑
	2011	Area 49: Adherence to guidance on **award fee contracts** could improve agencies' use of award fees to produce savings.	●
	2011	Area 50: Agencies aimed to save at least $3 billion by continued disposal of **unneeded federal real property.**	Consolidated or other
	2011	Area 51: Improved cost analyses used for making **federal facility ownership and leasing** decisions could save millions of dollars.	○

Mission	Annual report	Areas identified	Overall assessment
	2011	Area 52: The Office of Management and Budget's **IT Dashboard** reportedly has already resulted in savings and can further help identify opportunities to invest more efficiently in information technology.	●
	2011	Area 53: Increasing **electronic filing** of individual income **tax returns** could reduce IRS's processing costs and increase revenues by hundreds of millions of dollars.	◑
	2011	Area 54: Using **return on investment** information to better target IRS enforcement could reduce the tax gap; for example, a 1 percent reduction would increase tax revenues by $3.8 billion.	◑
	2011	Area 55: Better management of **tax debt collection** may resolve cases faster with lower IRS costs and increase debt collected.	◑
	2011	Area 56: Broadening IRS's authority to correct **simple tax return errors** could facilitate correct tax payments and help IRS avoid costly, burdensome audits.	○
	2011	Area 57: Enhancing **mortgage interest information** reporting could improve tax compliance.	○
	2011	Area 58: More information on the types and uses of canceled debt could help IRS limit revenue losses of **forgiven mortgage debt**.	◑
	2011	Area 59: Better information and outreach could help increase revenues by tens or hundreds of millions of dollars annually by addressing overstated **real estate tax deductions**.	◑
	2011	Area 60: Revisions to content and use of **Form 1098-T** could help IRS enforce higher education requirements and increase revenues.	◑
	2011	Area 61: Many options could improve the tax compliance of **sole proprietors** and begin to reduce their $68 billion portion of the tax gap.	◑
	2011	Area 62: IRS could find additional **businesses not filing tax returns** by using third-party data, which show such businesses have billions of dollars in sales.	◑
	2011	Area 63: Congress and IRS can help **S corporations** and their shareholders be more tax compliant, potentially increasing tax revenues by hundreds of millions of dollars each year.	◑
	2011	Area 64: IRS needs an agencywide approach for addressing tax evasion among the at least 1 million **networks of businesses** and related entities.	◑
	2011	Area 65: Opportunities exist to improve the targeting of the $6 billion **research tax credit** and reduce forgone revenue.	○
	2011	Area 66: Converting the **new markets tax credit** to a grant program may increase program efficiency and significantly reduce the $3.8 billion 5 years revenue cost of the program.	○
	2011	Area 67: Limiting the tax-exempt status of certain **governmental bonds** could yield revenue.	○

Mission	Annual report	Areas identified	Overall assessment
	2011	Area 68: Adjusting **civil tax penalties** for inflation potentially could increase revenues by tens of millions of dollars per year, not counting any revenues that may result from maintaining the penalties' deterrent effect.	◑
	2011	Area 69: IRS may be able to systematically identify **nonresident aliens** reporting unallowed tax deductions or credits.	●
	2011	Area 70: Tracking **undisbursed balances** in **expired grant accounts** could facilitate the reallocation of scarce resources or the return of funding to the Treasury.	●
	2012	Area 41: **General Services Administration Schedules Contracts Fee Rates:** Re-evaluating fee rates on the General Services Administration's Multiple Award Schedules contracts could result in significant cost savings government-wide.	●
	2012	Area 42: **U.S. Currency:** Legislation replacing the $1 note with a $1 coin would provide a significant financial benefit to the government over time.	○
	2012	Area 43: **Federal User Fees:** Regularly reviewing federal user fees and charges can help the Congress and federal agencies identify opportunities to address inconsistent federal funding approaches and enhance user financing, thereby reducing reliance on general fund appropriations.	○
	2012	Area 44: **Internal Revenue Service Enforcement Efforts:** Enhancing the Internal Revenue Service's enforcement and service capabilities can help reduce the gap between taxes owed and paid by collecting billions in tax revenue and facilitating voluntary compliance.	◑
	2013	Area 21: **Additional Opportunities to Improve Internal Revenue Service Enforcement of Tax Laws:** The Internal Revenue Service can realize cost savings and increase revenue collections by billions of dollars by, among other things, using more rigorous analyses to better allocate enforcement and other resources.	a
	2013	Area 23: **Agencies' Use of Strategic Sourcing:** Selected agencies could better leverage their buying power and achieve additional savings by directing more procurement spending to existing strategically sourced contracts and further expanding strategic sourcing practices to their highest spending procurement categories—savings of one percent from selected agencies' procurement spending alone would equate to over $4 billion.	a
	2013	Area 24: **Opportunities to Help Reduce Government Satellite Program Costs:** Government agencies could achieve considerable cost savings on some missions by leveraging commercial spacecraft through innovative mechanisms such as hosted payload arrangements and sharing launch vehicle costs. Selected agencies have reported saving hundreds of millions of dollars to date from using these innovative mechanisms.	a
Health	2011	Area 71: Preventing billions in **Medicaid improper payments** requires sustained attention and action by CMS.	◑
	2011	Area 72: Federal oversight of **Medicaid supplemental payments** needs improvement, which could lead to substantial cost savings.	○
	2011	Area 73: Better targeting of **Medicare's** claims review could reduce **improper payments**.	◑

Mission	Annual report	Areas identified	Overall assessment
	2011	Area 74: Potential savings in **Medicare's payment** for **health care**.	◑
	2012	Area 45: **Medicare Advantage Payment:** The Centers for Medicare & Medicaid Services could achieve billions of dollars in additional savings by better adjusting for differences between Medicare Advantage plans and traditional Medicare providers in the reporting of beneficiary diagnoses.	◑
	2012	Area 46: **Medicare and Medicaid Fraud Detection Systems:** The Centers for Medicare & Medicaid Services needs to ensure widespread use of technology to help detect and recover billions of dollars of improper payments of claims and better position itself to determine and measure financial and other benefits of its systems.	◑
	2013	Area 25: **Medicaid Prepayment Controls:** More widespread use of prepayment edits could reduce improper payments and achieve other cost savings for the Medicare program, as well as provide more consistent coverage nationwide.	a
	2013	Area 26: **Medicaid Supplemental Payments:** To improve the transparency of and accountability for certain high-risk Medicaid payments that annually total tens of billions of dollars, Congress should consider requiring the Centers for Medicare & Medicaid Services to take steps that would facilitate the agency's ability to oversee these payments, including identifying payments that are not used for Medicaid purposes or are otherwise inconsistent with Medicaid payment principles, which could lead to cost savings. GAO's analysis of providers for which data are available suggests that savings could be in the hundreds of millions, or billions, of dollars.	a
	2013	Area 27: **Medicare Advantage Quality Bonus Payment Demonstration:** Rather than implementing the Medicare Advantage quality bonus payment program specifically established by law, the Centers for Medicare & Medicaid Services is testing an alternative bonus payment structure under a broad demonstration authority through a 3-year demonstration that has design flaws, raises legal concerns, and is estimated to cost over $8 billion; about $2 billion could be saved if it were canceled for its last year, 2014.	a
Homeland security/law enforcement	2011	Areas 75 and 76: **DHS's management of acquisitions** could be strengthened to reduce cost overruns and schedule and performance shortfalls.	◑
	2011	Area 77: Validation of **TSA's behavior-based screening program** is needed to justify funding or expansion.	◑
	2011	Area 78: More efficient **baggage screening systems** could result in about $470 million in reduced TSA personnel costs over the next 5 years.	◑
	2011	Area 79: Clarifying availability of certain **customs fee collections** could produce a one-time savings of $640 million.	●
	2012	Area 47: **Border Security:** Delaying proposed investments for future acquisitions of border surveillance technology until the Department of Homeland Security better defines and measures benefits and estimates life-cycle costs could help ensure the most effective use of future program funding.	◑
	2012	Area 48: **Passenger Aviation Security Fees:** Options for adjusting the passenger aviation security fee could further offset billions of dollars in civil aviation security costs.	○

GAO-13-496T

Mission	Annual report	Areas identified	Overall assessment
	2012	Area 49: **Immigration Inspection Fee:** The air passenger immigration inspection user fee should be reviewed and adjusted to fully recover the cost of the air passenger immigration inspection activities conducted by the Department of Homeland Security's U.S. Immigration and Customs Enforcement and U.S. Customs and Border Protection rather than using general fund appropriations.	◑
	2013	Area 28: **Checked Baggage Screening:** By reviewing the appropriateness of the federal cost share the Transportation Security Administration applies to agreements financing airport facility modification projects related to the installation of checked baggage screening systems, the Transportation Security Administration could, if a reduced cost share was deemed appropriate, achieve cost efficiencies and be positioned to install a greater number of optimal baggage screening systems than it currently anticipates.	a
Income security	2011	Area 80: **Social Security** needs data on pensions from noncovered earnings to better enforce **offsets** and ensure benefit fairness, resulting in estimated $2.4-$2.9 billion savings over 10 years.	○
Information technology	2013	Area 29: **Cloud Computing:** Better planning of cloud-based computing solutions provides an opportunity for potential savings of millions of dollars.	a
	2013	Area 30: **Information Technology Operations and Maintenance:** Strengthening oversight of key federal agencies' major information technology investments in operations and maintenance provides opportunity for savings on billions in information technology investments.	a
International affairs	2011	Area 81: Congress could pursue several options to improve collection of **antidumping and countervailing duties.**	○
	2012	Area 50: **Iraq Security Funding:** When considering new funding requests to train and equip Iraqi security forces, Congress should consider the government of Iraq's financial resources, which afford it the ability to contribute more toward the cost of Iraq's security.	●
	2013	Area 31: **Tobacco Taxes:** Federal revenue losses were as much as $615 million to $1.1 billion between April 2009 and 2011 because manufacturers and consumers substituted higher-taxed smoking tobacco products with similar lower-taxed products. To address future revenue losses, Congress should consider modifying tobacco tax rates to eliminate significant tax differentials between similar products.	a
Social Services	2012	Area 51: **Domestic Disaster Assistance:** The Federal Emergency Management Agency could reduce the costs to the federal government related to major disasters declared by the President by updating the principal indicator on which disaster funding decisions are based and better measuring a state's capacity to respond without federal assistance.	○

Source: GAO.

[a] As of April 9, 2013, we have not assessed the 2013 areas identified.

Legend:

● = Addressed, meaning all actions needed in that area were addressed.

◑ = Partially addressed, meaning at least one action needed in that area showed some progress toward implementation, but not all actions were addressed.

○ = Not addressed, meaning none of the actions needed in that area were addressed or partially addressed.

Consolidated or other = actions were not assessed this year.

Appendix II: Opportunities for Potential Financial Benefits in 2011-2013 Annual Reports

Through our 2011-2013 annual reports, we have identified 162 areas in which greater efficiency and effectiveness of government operations could be gained. As we have previously reported, estimating financial benefits associated with implementing our suggested actions is difficult in some cases due to budget and performance data limitations. Furthermore, the amount of savings can depend on the extent to which the actions are taken. However, using available information, we were able to identify potential financial benefits of addressing some of the areas we identified. This information may help facilitate congressional decision making about the issues we identified.

Table 5 includes the areas for which we were able to estimate the potential financial benefits associated with implementing our suggested actions. Table 6 includes additional areas for which information was not available to develop precise estimates; however, using available information we were able to identify the range or magnitude of potential financial benefits.

Table 5: Estimated Financial Benefits for Certain Areas Included in 2011-2013 Annual Reports, as of March 15, 2013

Annual report	Areas identified
2011	**Farm Program Payments** (Area 35): Reducing farm program direct payments could result in savings from $800 million over 10 years to **up to $5 billion** annually depending on the policy choices made.
2013	**Crop Insurance** (Area 19): To achieve **up to $1.2 billion** per year in cost savings in the federal crop insurance program, Congress could consider limiting the subsidy for premiums that an individual farmer can receive each year, reducing the subsidy for all or high-income farmers participating in the program, or some combination of limiting and reducing these subsidies.
2011	**Federal Data Centers** (Area 15): Consolidating federal data centers provides an opportunity to improve government efficiency and achieve cost savings of **up to $3 billion** over 10 years.
2012	**Passenger Aviation Security Fees** (Area 48): Options for adjusting the passenger aviation security fee could further offset billions of dollars in civil aviation security costs by reducing the funds appropriated to address passenger aviation security. These options could increase fee collections from **about $2 billion to $10 billion** over 5 years.

GAO-13-496T

Annual report	Areas identified
2013	**Medicare Advantage Quality Bonus Payment Demonstration** (Area 27): Rather than implementing the Medicare Advantage quality bonus payment program specifically established by law, the Centers for Medicare & Medicaid Services is testing an alternative bonus payment structure under a broad demonstration authority through a 3-year demonstration that has design flaws, raises legal concerns, and is estimated to cost over $8 billion; **about $2 billion** could be saved if it were canceled for its last year, 2014.
2011	**Social Security Offsets** (Area 80): Social Security needs data on pensions from noncovered earnings to better enforce offsets and ensure benefit fairness, which could result in an **estimated $2.4 billion to $2.9 billion** savings over 10 years.
2011	**Oil and Gas Resources** (Area 45): Improved management of federal oil and gas resources could result in **approximately $2 billion** in additional revenue over 10 years.
2012	**U.S. Currency** (Area 42): Legislation replacing the $1 note with a $1 coin would provide a significant financial benefit of $4.4 billion over 30 years to the government, amounting to an average yearly discounted net benefit of **about $146 million**.
2013	**Tobacco Taxes** (Area 31): Federal revenue losses were **as much as $615 million to $1.1 billion** between April 2009 and 2011 because manufacturers and consumers substituted higher-taxed smoking tobacco products with similar lower-taxed products. To address future revenue losses, Congress should consider modifying tobacco tax rates to eliminate significant tax differentials between similar products.
2011	**Baggage Screening Systems** (Area 78): More efficient baggage screening systems could result in **about $470 million** in reduced Transportation Security Administration personnel costs over the next 5 years.
2013	**Checked Baggage Screening** (Area 28): By reviewing the appropriateness of the federal cost share the Transportation Security Administration applies to agreements financing airport facility modification projects related to the installation of checked baggage screening systems, the Transportation Security Administration could, if a reduced cost share was deemed appropriate, achieve cost efficiencies of up to **$300 million** by 2030 and be positioned to install a greater number of optimal baggage screening systems than it currently anticipates.
2013	**Agricultural Quarantine Inspection Fees** (Area 18): The United States Department of Agriculture's Animal and Plant Health Inspection Service could have achieved **as much as $325 million** in savings (based on fiscal year 2011 data, as reported in GAO's March 2013 report) by more fully aligning fees with program costs; although the savings would be recurring, the amount would depend on the cost-collections gap in a given fiscal year and would result in a reduced reliance on U.S. Customs and Border Protection's annual Salaries and Expenses appropriations used for agricultural inspection services.
2012	**Border Security** (Area 47): Delaying proposed investments for future acquisitions of border surveillance technology until the Department of Homeland Security better defines and measures benefits and estimates life-cycle costs could help ensure the most effective use of future program funding. U.S. Customs and Border Protection requested **$242 million** to fund the new Plan for fiscal year 2012.

Annual report	Areas identified
2012	**Immigration Inspection Fee** (Area 49): The air and sea passenger immigration inspection user fee should be reviewed and adjusted to fully recover the cost of the air and sea passenger immigration inspection activities conducted by the Department of Homeland Security's U.S. Immigration and Customs Enforcement and U.S. Customs and Border Protection rather than using general fund appropriations; In 2011 this could have resulted in a reduction of **about $178 million** in appropriated funds used for inspection services.
2013	**Combat Uniforms** (Area 2): The Department of Defense's fragmented approach to developing and acquiring uniforms could be more efficient, better protect service members, and result in **up to $82 million** in development and acquisition cost savings through increased collaboration among the military services.
2012	**Auto Recovery Office** (Area 39): Unless the Secretary of Labor can demonstrate how the Auto Recovery Office has uniquely assisted auto communities, Congress may wish to consider prohibiting the Department of Labor from spending any of its appropriations on the Auto Recovery Office, thereby saving **up to $1.2 million** per year.

Source: GAO.

Table 6: Range or Magnitude of Potential Financial Benefits for Certain Areas Included in 2011-2013 Annual Reports, as of March 15, 2013

Annual report	Areas identified
	Category: Defense
2011	**Overseas Military Presence** (Area 36): The Department of Defense should assess costs and benefits of overseas military presence options before committing to costly personnel realignments and construction plans, thereby possibly saving **billions of dollars**.
2011	**DOD's Spare Parts Inventory** (Area 39): More efficient and effective management could limit future costs of DOD's spare parts inventory by **billions of dollars**.
2011	**Tactical Wheeled Vehicles** (Area 6): A department-wide acquisition strategy could reduce DOD's risk of costly duplication in purchasing Tactical Wheeled Vehicles. Reducing the number of joint light tactical vehicles DOD procures could result in **billions of dollars** of cost savings.
2011	**Corrosion Protection** (Area 41): Improved corrosion prevention and control practices could help DOD avoid **hundreds of millions of dollars** in unnecessary costs.
2011	**DOD's Military Medical Command Structures** (Area 2): Realigning the Department of Defense's military medical command structures and consolidating common functions could increase efficiency and result in projected savings in the hundreds of **millions of dollars**.

GAO-13-496T

Annual report	Areas identified
2012	**Defense Headquarters** (Area 34): To further reduce overhead-related costs in light of the recent changes in DOD's strategic priorities, DOD should continue to examine opportunities to consolidate or eliminate military commands that are geographically close or have similar missions, and to seek further opportunities to centralize administrative and command support services, functions or programs. Since we made our recommendation, DOD has set targets to save **several hundred million dollars** by 2017 through a range of planned headquarters-efficiency measures. However, in some cases the specific actions to achieve these savings have not yet been identified.
2012	**Military Health Care Costs** (Area 36): To help achieve significant projected cost savings of **millions of dollars** and other performance goals, the Department of Defense needs to complete, implement, and monitor detailed plans for each of its approved health care initiatives.
2013	**Joint Basing** (Area 20): The Department of Defense needs an implementation plan to guide joint bases to achieve **millions of dollars** in cost savings and efficiencies anticipated from combining support services at 26 installations located close to one another.
	Category: Improper Payments
2011	**Government-wide Improper Payments** (Area 46): Efforts to address government-wide improper payments, including Medicare and Medicaid, estimated **at $108 billion in 2012**, could result in significant cost savings.
	Category: Federal Contracting
2011	**Competition for Federal Contracts** (Area 47): Promoting competition for the over $500 billion in federal contracts could potentially save **billions of dollars** over time.
2011	**Strategic Sourcing** (Area 48): Applying strategic sourcing best practices throughout the federal procurement system could save billions of dollars annually.
2013	**Agencies' Use of Strategic Sourcing** (Area 23): Selected agencies could better leverage their buying power and achieve additional savings by directing more procurement spending to existing strategically sourced contracts and further expanding strategic sourcing practices to their highest spending procurement categories—savings of one percent from selected agencies procurement spending alone would equate to **over $4 billion**.
2013	**Opportunities to Help Reduce Government Satellite Program Costs** (Area 24): Government agencies could achieve considerable cost savings on some missions by leveraging commercial spacecraft through innovative mechanisms such as hosted payload arrangements and sharing launch vehicle costs. Selected agencies have reported saving **hundreds of millions of dollars** to date from using these innovative mechanisms.
	Category: Information Technology
2011	**IT Dashboard** (Area 52): OMB's IT Dashboard contributed to **billions of dollars** in reported savings and can further help identify opportunities to invest more efficiently in information technology.
2012	**Navy's Information Technology Enterprise Network** (Area 38): Better informed decisions to ensure a more cost-effective acquisition approach for the Navy's Next Generation Enterprise Network could result in **billions of dollars** in cost savings.

Annual report	Areas identified
2013	**Information Technology Operations and Maintenance** (Area 30): Strengthening oversight of key federal agencies' major information technology investments in operations and maintenance provides an opportunity for **billions of dollars** in savings.
2011	**Enterprise Architecture** (Area 14): Well defined and implemented enterprise architectures in federal agencies can lead to consolidation and reuse of shared services and elimination of antiquated and redundant mission operations, which can result in significant cost savings. For example, the Department of the Interior demonstrated that it had used enterprise architecture to modernize agency IT operations and avoid costs through enterprise software license agreements and hardware procurement consolidation, resulting in financial savings of **at least $80 million**. In addition, Health and Human Services will achieve savings and cost avoidance of **over $150 million** between fiscal year 2011 to 2015 by leveraging its EA to improve its telecommunications infrastructure.
2012	**Information Technology Investment Management** (Area 19): Identifying and consolidating potentially duplicative IT investments at the Departments of Defense and Energy could result in **millions of dollars** in cost savings.
2013	**Cloud Computing** (Area 29): Better planning of cloud-based computing solutions provides an opportunity for potential savings of **millions of dollars**.
2013	**Geospatial Investments** (Area 11): Better coordination among federal agencies that collect, maintain, and use geospatial information could help reduce duplication of geospatial investments and provide the opportunity for potential savings of **millions of dollars**.
	Category: Tax Expenditures
2011	**Research Tax Credits** (Area 65): Opportunities exist to improve the targeting of the **$6 billion research tax credit** and reduce forgone revenue.
2011	**New Markets Tax Credit** (Area 66): Converting the new markets tax credit to a grant program could decrease the 35 percent to 50 percent difference between the cost of the credit to the Treasury (**$4.3 billion over 5 years**) and the amount actually received by projects being subsidized.
2011	**Ineffective Tax Expenditures and Redundancies** (Area 17): Periodic reviews could help ineffective tax expenditures and redundancies in related tax and spending programs, potentially reducing revenue losses by **billions of dollars**.
2011	**Governmental Bonds** (Area 67): As Congress considers whether tax-exempt governmental bonds should be used for professional sports stadiums that are generally privately used, it may also wish to consider whether other facilities, including hotels and golf courses, that are privately used should continue to be financed with tax-exempt governmental bonds. Implementing this suggestion could increase revenue because the interest earned by investors who purchase tax bonds is generally excluded from federal income taxes, resulting in **billions of dollars** annually in federal revenue losses.
2011	**Real Estate Tax Deductions** (Area 59): Better information and outreach could help increase revenues by tens or **hundreds of millions of dollars** annually by addressing overstated real estate tax deductions.

GAO-13-496T

Annual report	Areas identified
	Category: Tax Gap
2011-12	**Internal Revenue Service Enforcement** (Area 54, 2011; Area 44, 2012): More complete analysis of return on investment—revenue collected including from improvements in voluntary compliance compared to costs—across all of IRS's service and enforcement programs could help better target IRS's limited resources and reduce the $385 billion net tax gap. If service and enforcement improvements reduce the tax gap by 1 percent, the additional revenue would be about **$3.8 billion per year**. For example, expanding third-party information reporting on rental real estate service payments and service payments to corporations alone, as GAO has recommended, would increase revenues by an estimated **$5.9 billion over 10 years**. Other areas in which IRS could enhance enforcement include: • **Broad and specific math-error authority** (Area 56, 2011): Math error authority is statutory authority that allows IRS to correct certain errors on tax returns without a burdensome audit of the taxpayer. By granting either general authority or specific math error authority related to, for example, individual retirement accounts or the residential energy credit, IRS could improve compliance at low costs. • **Form 1098T (Area 60, 2011):** Every year millions of taxpayers claim billions of dollars of credits for post-secondary education tuition expenses. Revising the Form 1098 T to provide more complete information on qualified expenses could make it easier for IRS to ensure that taxpayers claim the correct amount. • **Businesses Not Filing Tax Returns** (Area 62, 2011): According to third-party information, businesses not filing tax returns have billions of dollars in sales. Better use of the third-party information to enforce filing requirements could ensure taxes are paid on income associated with such sales. • **Networks of Businesses** (Area 64, 2011): Some owners of related businesses use such networks to evade tax. Because there are at least 1 million such networks, an IRS-wide strategy to address network-based tax evasion could bring in additional enforcement revenue.
2011	**Better Management of Tax Debt Collection** (Area 55): Better management of tax debt collection may resolve cases faster with lower Internal Revenue Service costs and increase debt collected. The Internal Revenue Service has recognized that each year individuals do not pay **billions of dollars** of their acknowledged tax debts.
2011	**S Corporations Compliance** (Area 63): Better IRS guidance on S corporation basis and shareholder compensation could, potentially, increase taxes paid by **hundreds of millions of dollars** each year.
2011	**Electronic Filing of Individual Income Tax Returns** (Area 53): Increasing electronic filing of individual income tax returns could save the Internal Revenue Service **millions of dollars** in processing costs by avoiding transcription.
	Category: Other
2012	**Medicare and Medicaid Fraud Detection Systems** (Area 46): The Centers for Medicare & Medicaid Services need to ensure widespread use of its fraud detection systems to better position itself to determine and measure progress toward achieving the **$21 billion** in financial benefits that the agency projected as a result of implementing these systems.

Annual report	Areas identified
2012	**Spectrum Management** (Area 13): Enhanced coordination of federal agencies' efforts to manage radio frequency spectrum and an examination of incentive mechanisms to foster more efficient spectrum use may aid regulators' attempts to jointly respond to competing demands for spectrum while identifying valuable spectrum that could be auctioned for commercial use. Past auctions of spectrum have generated **tens of billions of dollars** for the U.S. Treasury.
2012	**Medicare Advantage Payment** (Area 45): The Centers for Medicare & Medicaid Services could achieve billions of dollars in additional savings by better adjusting for differences between Medicare Advantage plans and traditional Medicare providers in the reporting of beneficiary diagnoses. We estimated that cumulatively across the three years from 2010 to 2012, a more accurate adjustment could have saved between **$3.2 billion to $5.1 billion**.
2012	**Domestic Disaster Assistance** (Area 51): Providing a more comprehensive assessment of a jurisdiction's capability to respond to and recover from a disaster without federal assistance to support disaster declaration decisions could save **billions of dollars**. As of January 31, 2012, FEMA anticipated that when all 539 approved disaster declarations designated during fiscal years 2004-2011 are closed, total Disaster Relief Fund obligations will be about $91.5 billion. GAO's analysis of FEMA's anticipated obligations for 508 declarations with Public Assistance during fiscal years 2004-2011 shows that 44 percent and 25 percent would not have met the indicator used to support declaration decisions if it had been adjusted for increases in personal income and inflation, respectively, since 1986.
2013	**Medicaid Supplemental Payments** (Area 26): To improve the transparency of and accountability for certain high-risk Medicaid payments that annually total tens of billions of dollars, Congress should consider requiring the Centers for Medicare & Medicaid Services to take steps that would facilitate the agency's ability to oversee these payments, including identifying payments that are not used for Medicaid purposes or are otherwise inconsistent with Medicaid payment principles, which could lead to cost savings. GAO's analysis for providers for which data are available suggests that savings could be in the **hundreds of millions, or billions, of dollars**.
2011	**FEMA Grants** (Area 26): Congress may wish to consider limiting preparedness grant funding to maintaining existing capabilities (as determined by the Federal Emergency Management Agency) until FEMA completes a national preparedness assessment of capabilities gaps at each level based on tiered, capability-specific performance objectives to enable prioritization of grant funding. In April 2011, Congress reduced funding for FEMA preparedness grants by **$875 million** from the amount requested in the President's fiscal year 2011 budget. In December 2011, Congress reduced funding for FEMA preparedness grants by **$1.28 billion** from the amount requested in the President's fiscal year 2012 budget.
2012	**Overseas Administrative Services** (Area 20): U.S. government agencies could lower the over **$2 billion** administrative cost of their operations overseas by increasing participation in the International Cooperative Administrative Support Services system and by reducing reliance on American officials overseas to provide these services.
2011	**Behavior Based Screening** (Area 77): Upon completion of the validation effort, Congress may also wish to consider the study's results— including the Screening of Passengers by Observation Techniques (SPOT) program's effectiveness in using behavior-based screening techniques to detect terrorists in the aviation environment—in making future funding decisions regarding the program. Depending on the results of DHS's validation effort and Congressional action, savings over the next 5 years could total tens of **millions of dollars**.

Annual report	Areas identified
2011	**Civil Tax Penalties** (Area 68): Adjusting civil tax penalties for inflation potentially could increase revenues by **tens of millions of dollars** per year, not counting any revenues that may result from maintaining the penalties' deterrent effect.
2011	**Federal Facility Ownership and Leasing** (Area 51): Improved cost analysis used for making federal facility ownership and leasing decisions could save **millions of dollars**.
2013	**Catfish Inspection** (Area 1): Repealing provisions of the 2008 Farm Bill that assigned U.S. Department of Agriculture's Food Safety and Inspection Service responsibility for examining and inspecting catfish and for creating a catfish inspection program would avoid duplication of already existing federal programs and could save taxpayers **millions of dollars** annually without affecting the safety of catfish intended for human consumption.
2011	**Excess Uranium Inventories** (Area 40): Marketing the Department of Energy's excess uranium could provide **substantial revenue** to the government.

Source: GAO.